Contents

A WORLD OF PRINT

EVEN IN THIS AGE OF COMPUTERS, TELECOMMUNICATIONS AND THE INFORMATION SUPERHIGHWAY, PRINTED TEXT AND PICTURES STILL CARRY MOUNTAINS OF INFORMATION AROUND THE WORLD. EVERY DAY, OUR LIVES ARE FLOODED BY PRINTED MATTER.

We use printed material from the moment we wake up until the moment we go to sleep. See how far through the day you can get without looking at something printed. Don't look at your alarm clock – the numbers on the dial are probably printed. Don't brush your teeth or use any perfume, deodorant or make-up, because the names, ingredients and instructions on the bottles, tubes and cans are printed. Don't read a newspaper, magazine or comic – they're printed too. Don't turn on a radio, because the station names and frequencies, and the labels on the controls, are printed. Don't play a tape or CD, because the labels are printed. And when you go out, don't look up at any road signs and don't look into any shop windows. It's impossible to avoid printed words and images.

SPREADING THE NEWS

Every day, newspapers provide us with a window on the most important events all over the world. Magazines entertain and inform us. Advertisements encourage us to buy products and services.

Newspapers, magazines and books are important because they hold people's thoughts. They are a form of one-way communication with people we will probably never meet. A library is a magical place. It's a storehouse of the thoughts, beliefs, hopes, fears and experiences of thousands of people, most of whom live far away and many of whom died long ago.

Some primitive societies do not use the printed word. Instead, people pass on their history, events and beliefs by word of mouth. They tell stories, which are passed down from generation to generation. However, there is no way of knowing how much a story has changed in the telling. A piece of printed text written 2000 years ago by someone who witnessed a battle tells the same story in the same words today as it did the day it was written. And it will tell the same story, in the words of the person who wrote it, to anyone who reads it a thousand years, 10,000 years, or 100,000 years from now.

Communications Close-up

Books and Newspapers

IAN GRAHAM

Published by Evans Brothers Limited
2A Portman Mansions
Chiltern Street
London
W1M 1LE

First published in 2000
Printed in Hong Kong.

Designer: Simon Borrough
Editor: Nicola Barber
Illustrations: Richard Morris, Hardlines

British Library Cataloguing in Publication Data

Graham, Ian, 1953-
Books & newspapers. - (Communications close-up)
1. Printing - Technological innovations - Juvenile literature 2. Book design - Juvenile literature 3. Newspapers - Juvenile literature
I. Title
686

ISBN 0237519836

Acknowledgements
Cover and page 6 Alex Bartel/Science Photo Library **page 7** Powerstock Photo Library/Zefa **page 8** (top) Kip Peticolas/ Fundamental Photos/Science Photo Library (bottom) Heidelberg Harris **page 11** With thanks to Gravure Graphics Ltd **page 12** Gary Gladstone/Image Bank **page 13** Peter Scholey/Robert Harding Picture Library **page 14** Bernard Roussel/ Image Bank **page 16** (middle left) Simon Fraser/Science Photo Library (middle right) Topham Picture Point **page 17** (top) Chris Close/ Image Bank (bottom) Deep Light Productions/Science Photo Library **page 18 and 19** With thanks to Aylesford Newsprint Ltd CDRom **page 20** With thanks to Keane Graphic Products Ltd **page 21** Dr Jeremy Burgess/Science Photo Library **page 22** Leonard Lessin, Peter Arnold Inc./Science Photo Library **page 23** Last Resort Picture Library **page 25** The National Trust Photo Library **page 26** Malcolm Piers/Image Bank **page 27** (top) Alecto Historical Editions /Bridgeman Art Library (middle) With thanks to the Fisher SPACE PEN Co. **page 28** Vo Trung/Eurelios/Science Photo Library **page 29** (top right) Powerstock Photo Library (bottom) Powerstock **page 31** (bottom left) Robert Francis/Robert Harding Picture Library (bottom right) Lowe Paul/Magnum cover pic from Film... **page 32** Paul Shambroom/ Science Photo Library **page 33** Jerry Mason/Science Photo Library **page 34** George Bernard/Science Photo Library **page 35** James King-Holmes/Science Photo Library **page 36** Power Stock **page 37** Last Resort Picture Library **page 38** Rolf Richardson/Robert Harding Picture Library **page 39** D. Vo Trung/Eurelios/Science Photo Library **page 40** Tom Van Sant, Geosphere Project/Planetary Visions/Science Photo Library **page 41** With thanks to Autodesk UK Ltd

At the Financial Times *printing press in London, the lights burn late into the night as the presses roll to print the newspaper.*

Libraries are storehouses of facts, figures, events, explanations, experiences, stories and memories – all printed. Without printing, books would have to be written by hand and they would be far too precious for the general public to handle and read.

If printed matter is to last thousands of years, it has to be looked after. All documents and inks suffer from decay and deterioration of one sort or another. Some last longer than others, depending on what they are made from and how they are kept. Print conservation has developed into an important branch of science practised in museums, libraries and archives all over the world. And, of course, the development of digital information storage means that all sorts of documents are being converted into digital form and stored in computers, where some of them can be accessed via the World Wide Web.

History links

THE FIRST NEWSPAPERS

A daily news-sheet was printed in Rome from about 59BC. It was called *Acta Diurna*, which means *Daily Events*. The first printed newspaper began in China in about AD700. The first modern European newspaper was the *Nieuwe Tijdingen* (*New Tidings*), printed in Antwerp from 1605.

PRINTING METHODS

THERE ARE THREE MAIN PRINTING METHODS IN USE TODAY: LETTERPRESS, GRAVURE AND LITHOGRAPHY. THE MOST WIDELY USED IS LITHOGRAPHY, WHICH ACCOUNTS FOR ROUGHLY HALF OF ALL PRINTING.

Lithographic printing relies on the fact that oil (top) and water (below) do not mix.

Pour a few drops of oil, for example cooking oil or olive oil, into a glass of water and see what happens. The water and oil don't mix. How ever much you stir them, blobs of oil eventually rise to the surface and join together, forming a separate layer on top of the water. Lithography depends on the different properties of water and oil-based printing ink to print from a perfectly flat printing plate. The printing area is on the same level as the non-printing area. The only difference between them is that the printing area is greasy, while the non-printing area is wet. The grease on one area and the water on the other do not mix.

MAKING PLATES

An image of the text and pictures to be printed is applied to the aluminium printing plate photographically, a process called photolithography

This offset litho printer is computer controlled.

(meaning 'writing with light'). The plate is then treated chemically so that when the plate is moistened, the printing area will repel the water. Then, when printing ink is applied to the plate, it sticks only to the dry parts.

To print a colour image, four separate plates are prepared. The yellow, cyan (blue), magenta (red) and black parts of an image are printed on top of each other (see page 15). Colour lithographs are also called chromolithographs or oleographs.

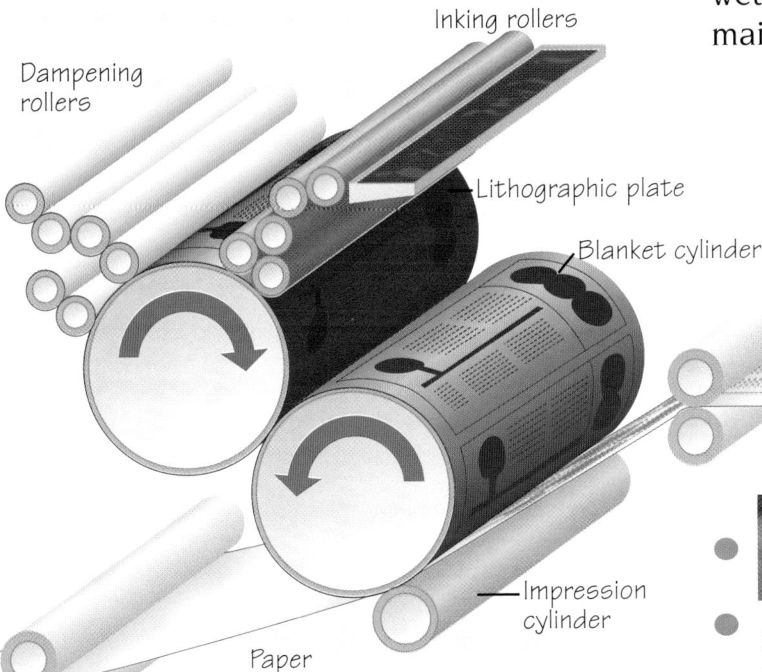

Ink-covered cylinders coat the lithographic printing plate with ink. As the plate turns, it transfers its image to the blanket cylinder, which prints the image on the paper.

OFFSET LITHO

The best-quality lithographic prints are made individually by hand, by a skilled printer. But most modern, commercial lithographic printing is done using an offset litho press. Offset presses transfer the image from the plate on to one or more cylinders before it is applied to the paper. Offset litho presses range in size from the small duplicating machines used to print short runs (small numbers) of brochures, to giant machines used to print thousands of books, magazines or newspapers.

GELATIN PRINTING

Collotype, or photogelatin, printing is a variation of lithography. A metal plate or a sheet of glass is coated with light-sensitive gelatin. An image is projected on to the gelatin, which hardens the most where the most light strikes it. Then the whole plate is dipped in water. The softer gelatin, where little light fell, soaks up lots of water, while the hardest gelatin, where most light fell, soaks up little water. Then the plate is inked. The harder gelatin accepts more ink than the softer, wetter gelatin. Collotype printing is mainly used for reproducing paintings.

History links

LETTERPRESS

Relief printing is the oldest printing method of all. A raised shape is covered with ink and then pressed against a sheet of paper. Some of the ink sticks to the paper and forms an image. Relief printing was used by the Ancient Chinese more than 1000 years ago, and it is still in use today – now known as letterpress. Nowadays, text and images are created on a plate photographically. The plate is covered by a film of light-sensitive emulsion and exposed to light through a negative of the text. The emulsion hardens where light hits it. The rest is washed away and the metal surface is deeply etched with acid, leaving the type standing higher than the rest of the surface.

GRAVURE

WHILE LETTERPRESS PRINTS FROM A RAISED IMAGE AND LITHOGRAPHY USES A FLAT PRINTING PLATE, GRAVURE PRINTS FROM A PLATE WHERE THE INKED PART OF THE PLATE IS LOWER THAN THE REST. IT IS AN EXAMPLE OF A PRINTING METHOD CALLED INTAGLIO.

Intaglio printing, or gravure, is a high-quality printing method. It uses a printing plate covered with thousands of tiny pits or cells. They act like microscopic ink-wells, holding the ink until it is transferred to the paper. The depth of the cells controls the intensity of the image on the paper because bigger cells hold more ink.

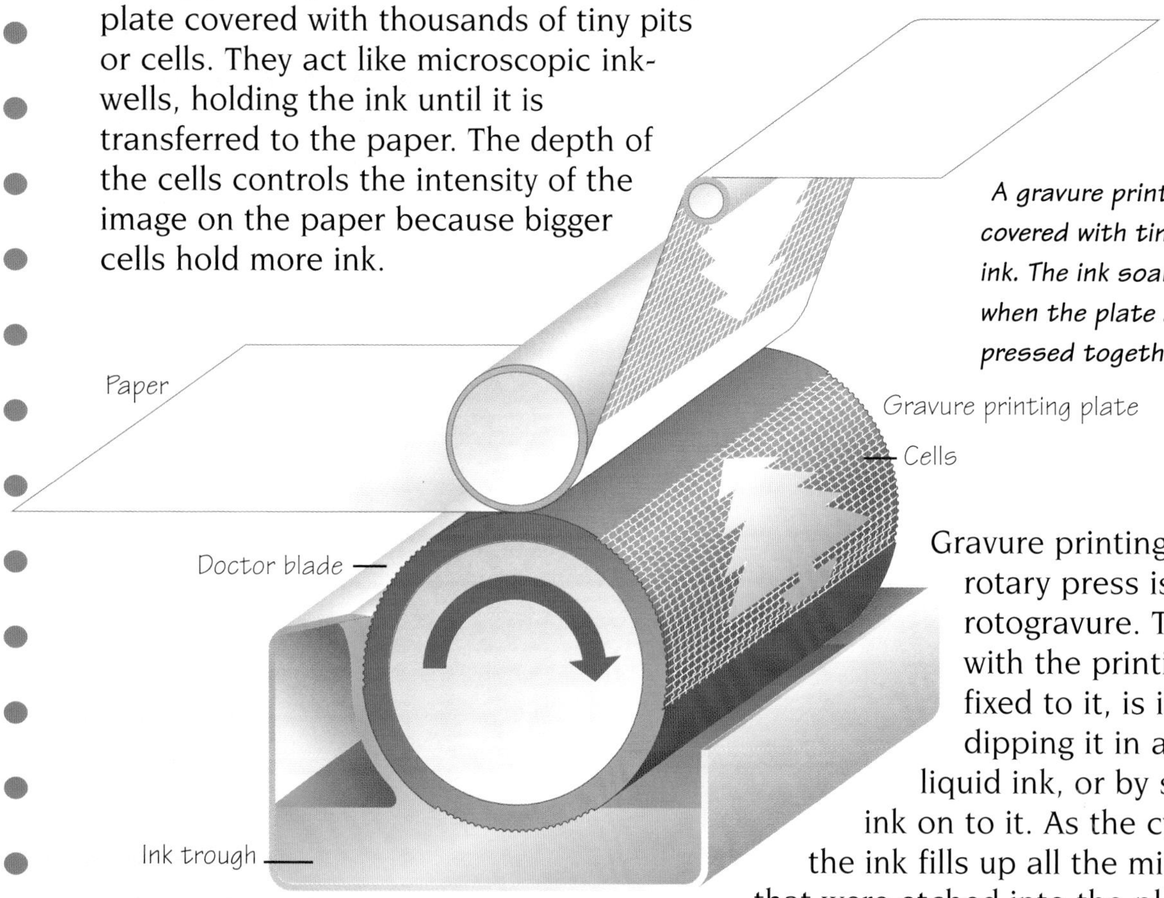

A gravure printing plate is covered with tiny pits filled with ink. The ink soaks into the paper when the plate and paper are pressed together.

Paper
Gravure printing plate
Cells
Doctor blade
Ink trough

Gravure printing using a rotary press is called rotogravure. The cylinder, with the printing plate fixed to it, is inked by dipping it in a trough of liquid ink, or by spraying the ink on to it. As the cylinder turns, the ink fills up all the minute cells that were etched into the plate. As the cylinder continues rotating, a steel strip called a doctor blade cleans ink off all the smooth, polished non-printing areas, leaving only the cells below the plate's surface full of ink. The cylinder is pressed directly on to the paper, which soaks up the ink, drawing it out of the cells. Then, as the impression cylinder continues to rotate, it picks up more ink, is cleaned by the doctor blade and prints again, and so on. Gravure presses use liquid ink that can be either oil-based or water-based.

MAKING CELLS

Gravure printing plates can be made photographically, or by engraving the plates directly under the control of a computer. The plate is usually made from steel with a copper coating, and it is etched with acid. After it has been etched, a plate intended for very long print runs is coated again with chromium so that it doesn't wear out too quickly.

A copper cylinder sits on a rack waiting to be loaded on to the engraving machine that will turn it into a printing plate.

This electronic gravure engraving machine has 14 engraving heads. Each head engraves one page on the cylinder by cutting metal away to form the cells that will hold the printing ink.

Engraved cylinders are lined up for the final stage of production. They are plated with a thin film of chromium metal to make them harder wearing so that they last longer.

HIGH-QUALITY PRINTING

Gravure printing plates are expensive to make – much more expensive than lithographic plates, which is why lithography is used more widely. Gravure printing is reserved for high-quality printing where cost is not the most important factor, for example, short print runs of fine-art prints, high-quality photographic books, advertising leaflets and some stamps. It is also used for very long runs, when the cost of the plates is more easily paid back, such as print runs of 300,000 or more for magazines, newspaper colour supplements, mail order catalogues, and specialised packaging for goods.

History links

SECRET PRINTING

Gravure printing was invented in the 19th century as a result of the work of two men. In 1862, J.W. Swan invented a material called carbon tissue, made from paper coated with gelatin, that was sensitive to light. In 1878, Karl Klic used carbon tissue to transfer an image on to a cylinder, which was then used to print the image. He kept his new printing process secret until 1903, when a worker in Klic's printing company revealed its details.

SPECIALIST PRINTING

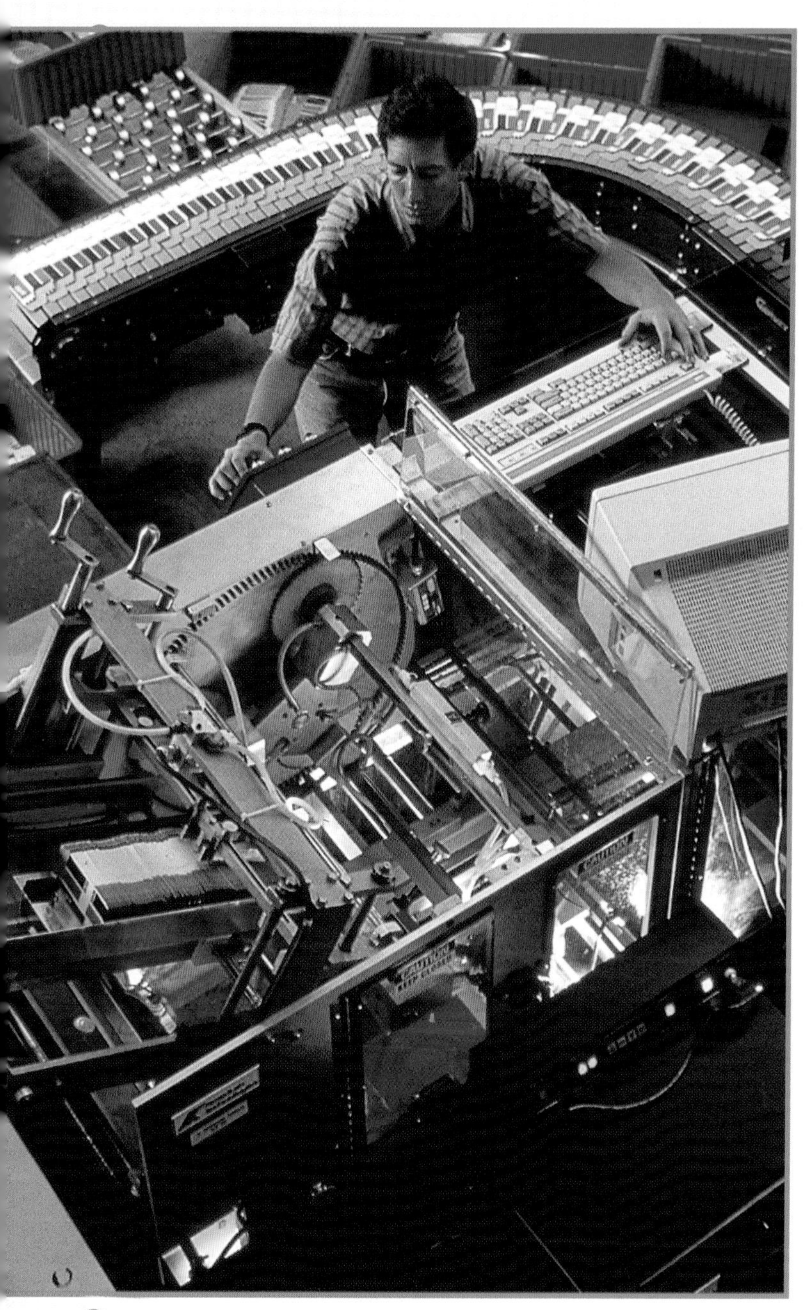

Product packages pass through a printing machine as the operator makes fine adjustments to the controls from the computer keyboard. Each package may have to go through several printing stages to build up a complicated design.

BOOKS, NEWSPAPERS AND MAGAZINES USED TO BE PRINTED ON PLAIN PAPER. BUT NOW, GLOSSY PAPERS, THICK CARD, A GREAT VARIETY OF PLASTICS AND EVEN METAL CAN BE USED TO MAKE PUBLICATIONS MORE ATTRACTIVE. THE PRINTING INDUSTRY HAS DEVELOPED MANY WAYS OF PRINTING ON THIS WIDE RANGE OF MATERIALS.

A greater variety of materials is used for printing books, newspapers, magazines and advertisements than ever before. You can find books and magazines with plastic or plastic-coated covers. To catch the customer's eye, the advertising industry produces text and graphics printed on almost every material imaginable. Ink normally dries by soaking into paper or card, but plastics and metals don't absorb liquids. The printing industry has developed a range of specialist printing techniques, including flexography, pad printing, inkjet printing and heat transfer decal printing to cope with these new materials.

FLEXOGRAPHY

Flexography is a high-speed printing method which uses quick-drying inks and a rubber printing plate. This printing plate is flexible enough to mould itself to the shape of the surface on to which it presses the ink. It can cope with non-absorbent surfaces and thick materials such as cardboard. The development of faster and cheaper plate-making methods using light-sensitive plastic has enabled flexographic printing presses to print newspapers and magazines, too. One advantage is that quick-drying flexographic inks don't come off on readers' hands like old-fashioned newsprint used to do.

JETS OF INK

Low-resolution (low-quality) inkjet printing is often used for jobs such as addressing magazines. The ink is sprayed on to the plastic magazine wrappers as they whizz past on a conveyor belt. High-resolution (high-quality) colour inkjet printing, which is much slower, is sometimes used to produce sample copies of images or documents for checking, before printing them in large numbers by a different method. The inkjet printer attached to a home computer produces each drop of ink only when it is needed, but some industrial inkjet printers produce a continuous spray of ink which is bent this way and that by magnetic fields to form letters and other symbols.

Link-ups

DATE-STAMPING

Inkjet printing is widely used in industry to print on fragile surfaces. This is because no part of the printing machine actually presses against the surface of the object to transfer the ink. For example, in some countries eggs are date-stamped by an inkjet printer, which sprays the date on to them as they pass through a packing machine.

PAD PRINTING

Computers have eliminated a lot of printing by enabling text and images to be created, stored and transmitted electronically – but computers themselves need the printing industry. A method called pad printing is used for printing the letters, numbers and other symbols that appear on a computer's keyboard. In pad printing, the image is etched into a plate called a cliché. This sunken image is then flooded with ink. A silicone pad presses on the cliché and picks up the ink, which becomes thicker as it starts to set. The pad is then pressed on to the object to be printed, transferring the thickened ink on to it.

Link-ups

HOT TRANSFERS

The heat-transfer decal process uses a hot stamp to lift an image, or decal, made from pigment or metal foil from a backing sheet. As a roll of decals (below) is pulled through the printing machine, the hot stamp picks up each decal off its backing sheet and presses it on to the surface to be printed. This heat transfer process can produce up to 2500 printed images per hour. Even hand-operated machines can work at 450 images per hour.

The symbols on a computer keyboard are printed using a process called pad printing.

Printing presses

Printing presses produce thousands, sometimes millions, of copies of the same publication. They have developed over hundreds of years into today's high-speed, high-tech printing machines.

Three main types of presses are used in the printing industry today – platen, flatbed and rotary. In a platen press, a sheet of paper is placed on a plate called the platen. The platen is raised up to press against the bed, which holds the frame of type that is to be printed. The platen moves down again, the printed paper is taken out, a new sheet is placed in position and the whole process starts again. An experienced operator can print up to about 5000 sheets per hour using a platen press.

In a flatbed press, the type or plate to be printed is locked into a flat surface, the flat bed. The paper is then pressed down on to it, either by a flat surface or by a heavy cylinder rolling over it. A flatbed press can produce up to about 4000 sheets per hour.

However, it is the rotary press that is mostly used today. It is the fastest of the three types and has mostly replaced platen and flatbed printing presses. Rotary presses print on paper that passes between two rollers, one of which carries a curved printing plate.

Newspaper presses

Newspapers are printed on web offset presses. Offset presses transfer the image from the printing plate on to cylinders called blankets, and the blankets then print the image on to the paper. The name 'web' refers to the continuous strip of paper that runs off a giant roll.

Web offset newspaper presses are huge machines operated by teams of skilled people. Blank paper is fed in at one end and complete newspapers come out at the other end. Ink-flow, paper tension, roller pressure and many other factors have to be continually monitored

The speed of paper through a newspaper printing press can be set very precisely using fingertip controls.

and adjusted to maintain the best print quality. Older presses were operated manually, but computer-controlled presses are standard today.

PRINTING IN COLOUR

Newspapers used to be printed entirely with black ink, but colour printing is now more usual. Colour printing is done in four stages, with four different colours of inks – yellow, cyan (blue), magenta (red) and black. Before something can be printed in colour, it has to be separated into four different images – one for each of the four colours. These four different images are called colour separations. A different printing plate is made for each colour. The paper passes through the press, having the four images printed on it, one after another.

THE FIRST PRINTING PRESSES

The presses that began the rapid spread of printing across Europe and around the world were built by Johann Gutenberg in Germany in the late 1440s. He developed movable type – individual metal letters and numbers that could be locked together in any order, in about 1440. The first printing press was set up in England, near Westminster Abbey in London, in 1477 by William Caxton. He learned how to use these printing presses in Germany.

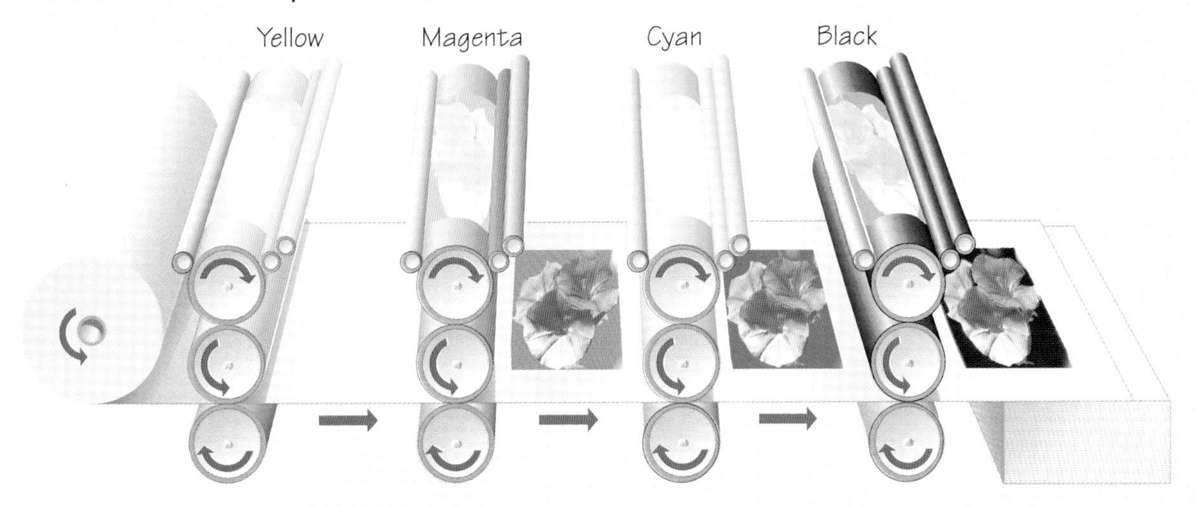

Colour printing is built up in stages. It is vital that the paper is held in exactly the right position or the colours will not line up accurately.

COMPUTER TO PLATE

Presses print from printing plates. Today, the plates are usually produced by a photographic method, using chemicals which harden when exposed to light. But the photographic stage of the plate-making process interrupts the flow of information from computer to paper. A development called computer-to-plate (CTP) eliminates this stage. In CTP, a computer scans a laser across a light-sensitive plate. The data stored in the computer's memory changes the strength of the laser beam as it scans back and forth, building up the image of the pages line by line. The plate is then treated chemically in the usual way to reveal the image and form the printing plate. The data has gone directly from the computer to the plate, saving time and improving image quality.

Making paper

Paper-making is a huge, global industry. Every day billions of newspapers and magazines are printed around the world. Every year, millions of books are printed, as well as countless advertisements, brochures, information sheets, catalogues and directories.

A timber mill (below) takes in logs that have been floated down-river and transforms them into bales of pulp for making paper (bottom).

Paper has been used for writing since about AD110 in China. The secret of making paper spread from China to Central Asia in about 750. By 900, it had reached Egypt and, 200 years later, Morocco. It then spread through Spain to France and, by the 1270s, it had travelled around the Mediterranean Sea to Italy. The first English paper mill was built in 1494.

From forest to page

Most paper is made from pulp, a thick soup of fibres. The pulp may be bleached to whiten it. Bales of dried pulp are sent to paper mills, where they are soaked in water, and pounded and stirred to break up the fibres even more. Dyes, binders, sealers and coating chemicals are added at this point to improve the paper's colour and its ability to accept ink.

Next, the pulp goes to the paper-making machine. There are two types – the Fourdrinier machine, named after the French brothers who invented it, and the cylinder machine. A Fourdrinier machine makes a continuous sheet of paper at up to 1000 metres per second by spreading pulp on a moving mesh screen. Some water drains out through the mesh and the rest is removed by driers. Finally, the paper is given a smooth finish by passing it through rollers. A cylinder machine forms thick paper or card on a mesh cylinder that rotates in a bath of pulp. The paper comes off the cylinder on to a conveyor belt that carries it away.

Sometimes, a wire pattern is pressed into paper before it dries, creating a thin area that looks paler when light shines through it – a watermark.

History links

A GRAVE SHORTAGE

In 1665, the Great Plague of London killed nearly 70,000 people. At that time, it was the custom to wrap bodies in cotton or linen shrouds before burial. But the huge number of deaths caused a serious shortage of rags, which were also needed for making paper. In 1666, the year of the Great Fire of London, the English government passed a law making it illegal to wrap bodies in cotton or linen, to protect the supply of rags for paper-making.

Wood pulp travels through a paper mill (left). It is heated and rolled to dry it out and smooth its surface. The finished paper is wound on to large rolls (below) and transported to printing works.

Pulp recipes

Paper-makers make different types of paper by changing the pulp recipe. And they do that by mixing pulps made from different fibres. The fibres come from ground-up wood, hemp, jute, bamboo, rice, cotton, grass, sugar cane, wheat and artificial materials such as nylon. Different papers have different properties. Paper for inkjet printing must prevent the liquid ink from spreading and forming a spidery image. Papers for glossy magazines are coated with starch and clay and then polished.

Electronic paper

Despite the abundance of portable computers, handheld computers, palm-tops and organisers, many people still prefer to write and draw using a pen and paper. Now, IBM has developed a system that allows people to write on paper with a pen and also have the information recorded digitally. The paper sits on an electronic panel. The pen contains a coil, which the panel detects so that it can follow the pen's movements. Everything drawn on the paper is stored in the panel's memory. This memory can hold up to 50 pages of writing before it has to be downloaded into a computer.

RECYCLING PAPER

NEWSPAPERS AND SOME MAGAZINES ARE PRINTED ON A TYPE OF PAPER CALLED NEWSPRINT. SOME OF THE MILLIONS OF NEWSPAPERS AND MAGAZINES THAT ARE THROWN AWAY EVERY DAY ARE NOW COLLECTED AND RECYCLED TO BE TURNED ONCE AGAIN INTO NEWSPRINT.

Newsprint is traditionally made from wood pulp. Most of it is made from ground up wood, called mechanical pulp or groundwood pulp. The rest is made from chemical pulp – ground-up wood cooked with chemicals. Replacing some of the wood pulp with recycled pulp from waste paper reduces both the amount of ground-up wood needed, and the amount of waste paper to be disposed of. It also saves energy. Recycling one million tonnes of used newspapers and magazines saves energy equivalent to 186,000 tonnes of oil.

Used magazines and newspapers are collected and brought to dumping point at the recycling centre.

THE RECYCLING PROCESS

The first stage in the recycling process is to pulp the used paper by stirring it up with water in a giant tank. The pulp is treated with chemicals such as caustic soda, hydrogen peroxide and sodium silicate to loosen the old ink from the paper fibres. A screening machine takes out pins, staples and other solid objects. Then a de-inking machine removes the ink by bubbling a soap solution through the pulp. The ink rises to the top of the liquid with the bubbles, forming a black froth that is skimmed off.

The paper is fed into a pulper to be broken down, and unwanted matter, such as string, is removed.

Now the clean pulp can be turned into new paper. The porridge-like paper soup is injected between two moving belts of plastic mesh so that excess water can drain away. The soggy, continuous sheet,

The pulp is forced through a series of filters to remove sand and grit.

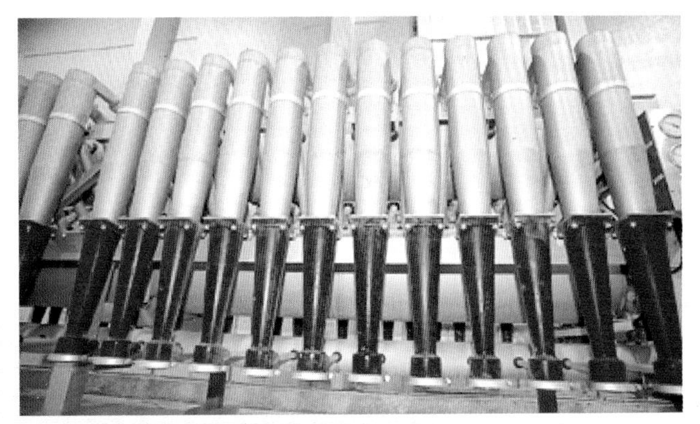

Other equipment removes more unwanted material: staples, plastics and bindings.

The pulp is pumped through a de-inking machine where the ink is floated off.

or web, of paper then passes through roller presses and over hot cylinders to drive off the rest of the water. The finished paper is wound on to reels weighing up to 40 tonnes each. Europe's biggest newsprint recycling plant produces 370,000 tonnes of newsprint per year.

The giant newsprint machine forms the pulp into paper and winds it into 9.2-metre reels (below).

SAVING ENERGY

Making newsprint requires large amounts of electricity and heat. Most power stations lose more than half of the heat produced by their fuel – it simply escapes into the atmosphere. Combined heat and power, or cogeneration, power stations save and use this waste heat, so they are ideal powerplants for paper mills. Their electricity powers the paper-making machinery, while the waste heat is used to make steam for the paper-drying cylinders. Cogeneration is not only more efficient, it is also kinder to the environment. A cogeneration plant fuelled by natural gas produces only half as much carbon dioxide, 90 per cent less nitrogen oxides and virtually no sulphur dioxide compared to a conventional power station. Carbon dioxide is a greenhouse gas, linked to global warming, and both nitrogen oxides and sulphur dioxide can cause acid rain. The largest paper mills have their own cogeneration powerplants.

The huge paper reels are cut and rewound according to customer requirements.

MAKING AN IMPRESSION

DIFFERENT PRINTING METHODS NEED DIFFERENT TYPES OF INK. THE FIRST INKS WERE MADE FROM NATURAL PIGMENTS USING MINERALS, PARTS OF PLANTS OR EVEN CRUSHED INSECTS. TODAY, PRINTERS HAVE AN EVER-GROWING RANGE OF SYNTHETIC INKS FROM WHICH TO CHOOSE.

Have a look at a few examples of printing – a newspaper, a glossy magazine, a telephone directory, a piece of wallpaper, a book, a CD label, a plastic washing-up bottle. The surfaces that carry the printing are all different. Some of the papers are very absorbent, while plastic labels and bottles absorb nothing. Newsprint, the paper used for printing newspapers, is thin and rough, while magazine paper is heavier and glossy. The printer has to choose the right ink for each job.

A modern printing ink has three main ingredients – vehicle, pigment and additives. The vehicle carries the ink colour on to the paper. It might be oil, water or a solvent such as alcohol. The pigment is the colour. Black ink is usually made from a pigment called carbon black. Coloured inks contain pigments made from a variety of chemical compounds. The additives are chemicals such as binders, fillers, thinners, stabilisers, retarders and hardeners that improve the ink's properties, perhaps making it flow easily, making it dry quickly or slowly, or making it resistant to fading in light.

Ink manufacture in a factory. Ink is delivered to commercial customers in large, 200-kilogram barrels.

HOW MUCH OIL AND COLOUR?

Most commercial printing inks are oil-based or solvent-based permanent inks, but the amount of oil or solvent varies according to what the ink is used for. Newsprint is very absorbent. When ink is applied to it, the oil sinks in to the paper, leaving the pigment on the surface. So, newsprint inks contain a lot of oil, perhaps up to 75 per cent of the total content.

Heat-set inks are liquid while they are cool, but set hard when their oil or water base is driven off by heat. Cold-set inks are liquid when hot and set when they are allowed to cool down. Moisture-set inks set on contact with water. Some inks dry to a high-gloss finish, while others dry to a dull, matt finish. Inks used in offset printing are more highly coloured than most, to compensate for the effect of transferring them on to a blanket cylinder before they are printed on to the paper. Flexographic printing uses quick-drying water-based or solvent-based inks. Gravure or rotogravure uses liquid ink, while offset litho printing uses ink in the form of a thick greasy paste. Pad printing uses inks with extremely high levels of pigment. Inkjet printing uses very thin, free-flowing inks.

Electric ink

One of the strangest new uses for ink is to carry an electric current. Electric circuits are normally made from electronic components fixed to a plastic or glass-fibre circuit board. Metal tracks on the board connect the components. Researchers at Brunel University, London, have succeeded in making circuits by printing them on to paper using a special ink that conducts electricity. Printing circuits like this cuts manufacturing costs – and it's friendlier to the environment.

History links

THE DEVELOPMENT OF INK

The ink used by early writers and printers was very different from the inks used today. It was thick and full of grit and sludge. This wasn't a problem for dip pens, but it clogged fountain pens, and it wouldn't stick to the metal type used in the first printing presses. In the 1440s, Johann Gutenberg developed an ink that would stick to metal, but a clean, permanent and effective fountain-pen ink that would leave a strong mark on paper without soaking into it too much wasn't developed until the 1860s.

Most circuit boards have metal lines, or tracks, stuck to them to carry electric currents. It is now possible to make circuits by printing electric tracks on to paper or cardboard with special ink.

SECURITY INKS

SOME INKS DO MORE THAN JUST MAKE A MARK ON PAPER. THEY HELP TO STOP IMPORTANT DOCUMENTS FROM BEING TAMPERED WITH OR COPIED. SECURITY INKS HAVE BECOME AN IMPORTANT PART OF THE PRINTING INDUSTRY.

Today, the widespread use of colour photocopiers, scanners and printers enables forgers and counterfeiters to copy important documents quite easily. A range of security inks has been developed to help combat forgery and fraud.

One way of combatting forgers is to use special inks or dyes that are hard to copy. This German 100 Deutschmark note has fluorescent markers which show up only in ultraviolet light.

FOILING SCANNERS

All scanners and photocopiers read the information on a document by scanning a bright light across it and measuring the strength and colour of the reflection that bounces back. A security ink can either stop a document from being scanned – or show that it has been scanned.

One type of security ink reflects particular ultraviolet and infrared wavelengths that cannot be picked up by scanners. However, these wavelengths are also invisible to the human eye, and these inks have to be viewed under a special light. Monochromic security inks change colour completely and permanently if they are scanned or copied, producing a colour change that is easily spotted. Other reactive inks change colour if heat is applied to them or if they are illuminated with a laser. They may not stop a document from being copied, but at least you will know that it has been copied.

Another type of security ink has a pearly finish that scatters light randomly in all directions in different colours. Even the best colour copier or printer can't reproduce that sort of sparkling surface effect. And by carefully controlling its chemical composition, an ink can be made to reflect a particular range of wavelengths, so that the ink has its own 'signature' when viewed under an infrared or ultraviolet light.

DISAPPEARING INK

Plastic cards that are used to pay for goods – credit cards, debit cards and cheque guarantee cards – have a special panel on the back for the cardholder's signature. This signature is used as a check for shop and bank staff that the person using the card is its real owner. This panel is usually overprinted using a special ink that is designed to show if the card has been tampered with. If anyone tries to remove the signature on the panel and write another one in its place, the overprinting disappears, or changes to read 'Void'.

ELECTRICITY AND MAGNETISM

Some security inks look like perfectly normal inks. A forger may produce a copy of a document that looks identical to the original. But the forger's ink lacks one vital property. The genuine ink is magnetic. Ink can also be made so that it conducts electricity. Magnetism and electrical conductivity are easily detected to verify that a document is genuine and not a forgery.

History links

STOPPING THE FORGERS

Multi-colour printing was invented in China in about 1107, mainly to make it more difficult for forgers to make counterfeit bank notes.

The panel on the back of a credit card is printed using inks that prevent the owner's signature from being replaced by a new one. Tampering with the card changes the ink, so a forgery is easy to spot.

Link-ups

Magnetic inks are used on cheques and bank drafts for two reasons. First, it enables forged cheques and bank drafts to be detected. Secondly, it enables information on genuine cheques and bank drafts to be read very quickly by Magnetic Ink Character Recognition (MICR). The paper passes under a detector which reads the printing by detecting its magnetism.

RESCUING PRINT

THE PRINTED WORD SEEMS TO BE PERMANENT AND UNCHANGING. MUSEUMS HOLD PRICELESS ILLUMINATED MANUSCRIPTS, BOOKS, PRIVATE LETTERS AND OTHER DOCUMENTS. SOME OF THEM ARE HUNDREDS OF YEARS OLD. SURPRISINGLY, MODERN PRINTED TEXTS ARE NOT NEARLY AS PERMANENT.

Open a book that's only 20 years old and it's quite likely that the edges of the pages are beginning to turn brown. If it's a paperback, some of the pages may actually fall out because the glue in the spine has become brittle. Thermal fax paper has the shortest lifespan of all. Images can fade and disappear from this paper within just a few months.

WHAT CAUSES THE DAMAGE?

Light, temperature, humidity, air pollution, insect pests and disasters such as flood and fire all shorten the lives of printed documents. If you open a cupboard or a drawer in a piece of antique furniture, the wood inside is often a richer, darker colour than the outside, because the outside has been bleached by sunlight. The dyes and pigments used in printing inks are bleached by light, too. The most damaging parts of light are the invisible ultraviolet wavelengths.

Another cause of damage is changing temperatures. If books are allowed to become too hot, chemical changes accelerate in the paper and inks, which break down all the more quickly. Fungi and moulds also flourish in higher temperatures. And a sudden drop in temperature can condense water vapour out of moist air, which makes fungi and moulds grow even faster.

ACID PAPER

Modern paper breaks down more quickly than older paper. Before about 1850, all paper was made from cotton or linen rag fibres with very few chemical additives. After about 1850, rags were gradually replaced by wood pulp. Wood-pulp paper is more acidic than rag paper – and it becomes even more acidic with age as the cellulose in the wood pulp breaks down. The paper turns brown and becomes brittle. Eventually, it turns to dust.

Salt (in sea air) and air pollution react chemically with paper. Book covers made from PVC (a type of plastic) give off a gas that is harmful to paper. Even wooden shelves can emit damaging acidic gases and moisture.

History links

TURNING THE TIDE

In 1966, the Italian city of Florence suffered serious flooding. Many of the city's historic museums and art galleries were inundated with water and mud. Florence's citizens dug through the mud with their hands to reach priceless books and documents so that conservation experts could get to work on them. The Florentine floods prompted many other museums, archives and galleries around the world to develop their own disaster plans.

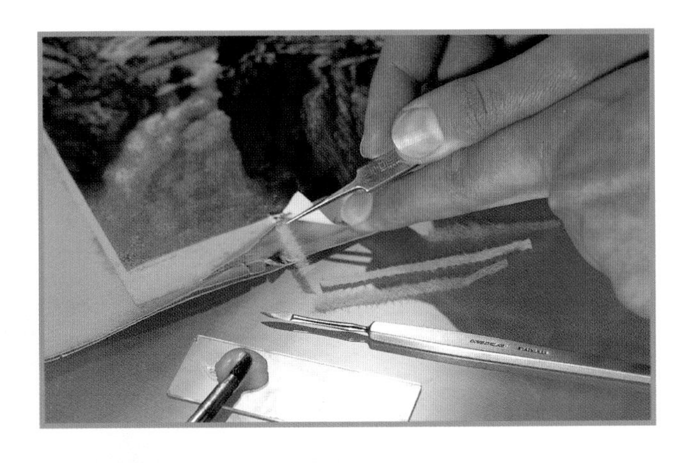

A conservator repairs tears in paper by pasting tissue paper over the tear. The tissue, called lens tissue, is fixed in place with arrowroot starch paste. The repair is almost invisible.

STOPPING THE ROT

Light, humidity and temperature are strictly controlled in libraries, archives and museums to minimise their damaging effects. Insect pests are controlled by pesticides. Acidic papers can be treated chemically to make them less acid. But if a disaster does happen, what can be done?

Waterlogged paper must be dried – but it has to be done carefully. The paper has to be kept flat, to stop it crinkling, and there must be lots of air movement to minimise mould growth – which starts within a few hours. Creases and folds are treated by moistening the paper to let the fibres 'relax' and then flattening and drying it. Solvents can take out oil, mud or smoke stains. But prevention is better than cure, and a lot less expensive, so document storage rooms are designed to minimise all of these risks.

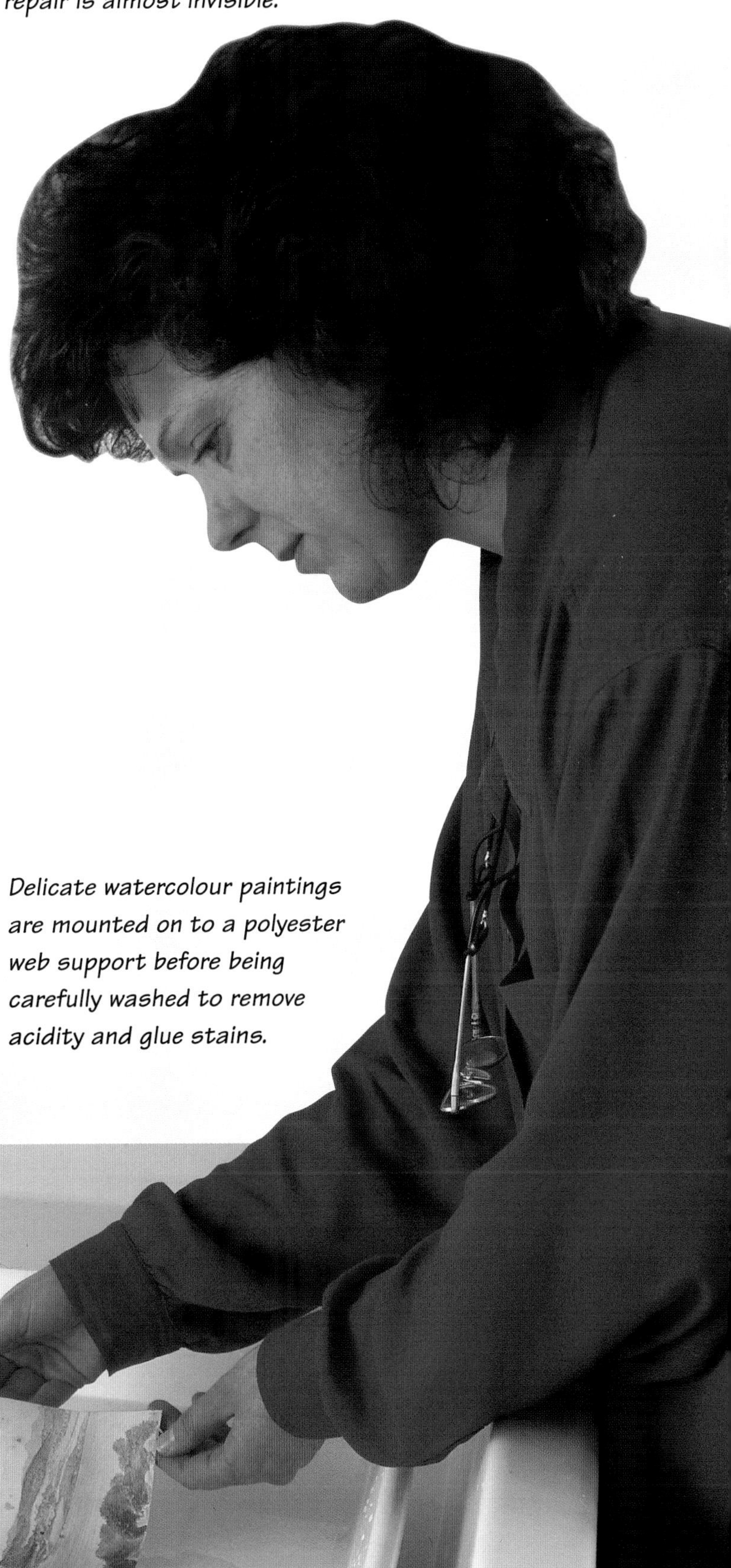

Delicate watercolour paintings are mounted on to a polyester web support before being carefully washed to remove acidity and glue stains.

Writing instruments

While enormous presses print our books, newspapers and magazines, and computer printers turn the contents of our computers' memories into 'hard copy', most of the time we put our thoughts on paper with much simpler writing tools.

Great books and memorable newspaper articles often begin with a pen and a sheet of paper. The pen remained virtually unchanged for more than 1000 years. Then, after the invention of the first practical fountain pen in the 1880s, there was an avalanche of technological development. Today, there is a wide choice of writing instruments.

On the ball

Liquid ink can run, blot and splash if it isn't handled carefully. Ballpoint pens use a thick, pasty ink that stays inside the pen. A thin tube carries the ink to the tip, where a pinhead-sized metal ball sits in a socket. When the pen is used, the ball rolls across the page and draws ink out of the tube. The ballpoint was invented by Lazlo Biró in the 1930s. It first became popular among World War II pilots because it didn't leak in the thin air at altitude.

A descendant of the ballpoint pen is the roller ball or rolling ball pen. It has a ball in its writing tip but, unlike a ballpoint pen, it uses a very runny ink and writes more like a fountain pen.

Soft-tip and felt-tip pens, introduced in the 1960s, also use a liquid ink. They draw it to the tip in a sort of controlled leak. The pen's felt or plastic tip is porous. Ink is drawn into it from a reservoir inside the pen by capillary attraction. As the pen is used, the loss of ink on to the paper draws more ink to the tip from the reservoir.

The space pen, used by US astronauts, relies on gas pressure to push the ink to the tip.

The tip of a ballpoint pen rolls smoothly across the paper leaving a trail of ink behind. The ink is like a thick jelly while it is inside the pen, and turns into a thinner liquid as it rolls on to the paper.

WRITING IN ZERO-GRAVITY

Turn a pen upside-down and see how long it keeps working if you try to write with it. Most pens need gravity to help pull the ink down to the nib or writing point. Without gravity acting in the right direction, they soon stop working. In an orbiting spacecraft, ink is weightless, so astronauts use pens that have been specially designed to work in space.

The Space Pen is the result of research costing two million US dollars. It can be used in zero gravity. It writes on almost any surface. It works in temperatures between -45°C and 120°C. It will even write under water. Its special ink is normally thick, like chewing gum.

But when the pen is being used, nitrogen gas inside the ink cartridge pushes the ink down to the tungsten carbide ball at the tip. The ball rotates and turns the ink to liquid. The property of being solid when stationary, and liquid when moving is called thixotropism. Tomato ketchup and non-drip paint are more down-to-earth examples of thixotropic materials!

History links

WHY PENKNIVES?

Small, folding pocket knives are called penknives because they were originally used for trimming a goose feather to make a quill pen. The quill nib wore out quickly and so a penknife was essential for keeping it in good shape.

Link-ups

HARD NIBS

Fountain-pen nibs made from gold have a tiny ball at the tip. The ball is made from a very hard material called iridium, because a soft gold nib on its own would wear down too quickly.

Text and Graphics

Books, newspapers, magazines, computer screens and signs are all designed to be attractive. They must also make the information they contain easy to read and understand.

Masthead

Headline

By-line

Lead story

Body text

Box rule

Dividing rule

Caption

DAILY CHRONICLE

VIRTUAL LIBRARY GOES ON-LINE

by Susan Knight

The British Library must, by law, hold at least one copy of every book published in Britain. Its shelves contain 20 million books. Managing a collection of this size, and giving people access to any book, is a vast task. And, with thousands more books being published every year, the job is getting more difficult all the time.

The Library is tackling this by transferring some of its books into a digital form. Once a book is digitised, it can be stored in a computer and whizzed down the information superhighway to any other computer screen anywhere in the world within a few minutes. Digitisation not only enables people all over the world to access books, it also allows people to see books and other documents that are too old, too fragile or too valuable to be handled for real.

Scanning for Internet access

SMART REVOLUTION

A plastic card with a computer chip embedded inside it is called a smart card. Some are memory cards containing a memory chip. Others are miniature computers with a central processing unit (CPU) as well as memory. Banks and shops that issue loyalty cards are beginning to update their magnetic strip cards to smart cards. Telephone companies issue smart cards for buying call time on their telephone services. And smart cards can be used instead of cash. The card is loaded with money which is transferred from a bank account. Each time the card is used to pay for something in a shop, it is inserted in a terminal and the amount of money stored in the card is reduced. Smart cards can also be used to hold identification information.

Setting out information clearly on a page, a computer screen or a sign involves choices of size, style, colour and position of text, images and backgrounds.

Page design

Open any newspaper and look at the arrangement of the text. The text sizes and styles, the sizes of the margins and the spacing between the lines are all chosen very carefully. The most important information is the headline or heading because it tells the reader what each story is about, so it is set in the largest type. The headline attracts the reader's attention first. Beneath it, there may be a line or two, set in smaller type. If the headline looks interesting, the reader may look at this introduction to find out a bit more about the story. Then comes the story itself, set in the smallest type.

A long story or feature article, or the text in an illustrated book, is usually broken up into shorter chunks. Each chunk has its own small heading, called a sidehead or crosshead. Photographs and illustrations usually have a short piece of text, called a caption, explaining what they show. In newspapers, the different stories on a page are usually separated by lines called rules, to make it easier to see where each story starts and ends. The designer or editor decides how big and what shape each photograph or illustration should be, so that the page has a certain style or look that is in keeping with the rest of the publication. Today, most books, newspapers and magazines are created using computers (see pages 30-1).

WHAT'S IN A COLOUR?

Look at any page. It is the colour photographs, drawings, computer graphics, lines, panels and boxes that bring it to life. Text is usually printed in black because it stands out clearly against a white page. Until the 1980s, most books, newspapers and magazines were printed totally in black and white. But the introduction of computer-controlled machines started a technology revolution in the printing industry that slashed the cost of colour printing, meaning that publishers could use colour almost wherever they wish.

Colour can be more than merely interesting or attractive. Colours can change your mood. Red tends to raise the blood pressure and make the pulse and breathing quicken. Orange and yellow have a similar but smaller effect. Blue and purple have the opposite effect.

The ways in which colours affect us are used in sign-making, to make us respond to them in the right way. Warning signs are often printed in red or orange. Information signs are often in blue.

History links

COMPUTER GRAPHICS

Computers use text and graphics to communicate with computer users. Early computers were controlled by typing in commands in the form of lines of text. It meant that computer users had to remember many different commands, and if they made the tiniest mistake in typing a command the computer wouldn't work. Then, in 1984, Apple launched the Macintosh computer which was controlled in a different way. The user moved a pointer around the screen using a mouse, and clicking the mouse button when the pointer was over a computer-generated drawing called an icon. The icons were designed so that they represented the job they did as clearly as possible. The computer did the rest.

GETTING INTO PRINT

COMPUTERS AND TELECOMMUNICATIONS HAVE REVOLUTIONISED THE PRODUCTION OF BOOKS, NEWSPAPERS AND MAGAZINES. THEY ENABLE INFORMATION OF ALL SORTS TO BE MOVED AROUND THE WORLD FASTER THAN EVER BEFORE, AND MAKE IT EASIER TO CREATE COLOURFUL AND EXCITING PUBLICATIONS.

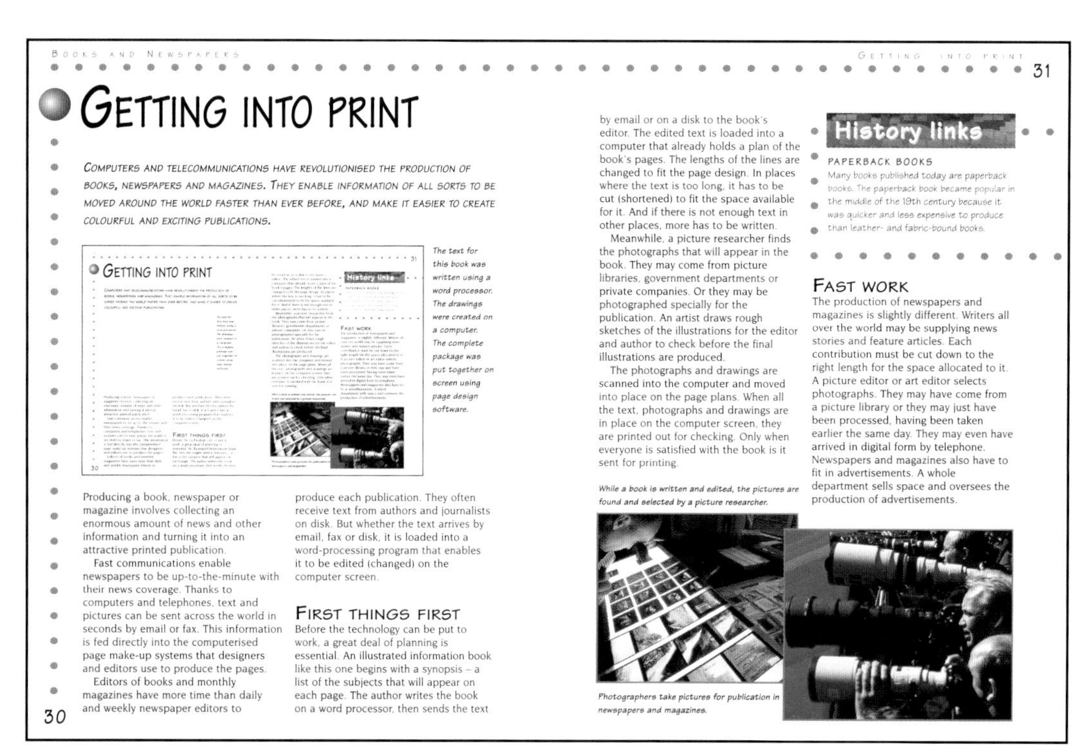

BOOKS AND NEWSPAPERS

GETTING INTO PRINT

COMPUTERS AND TELECOMMUNICATIONS HAVE REVOLUTIONISED THE PRODUCTION OF BOOKS, NEWSPAPERS AND MAGAZINES. THEY ENABLE INFORMATION OF ALL SORTS TO BE MOVED AROUND THE WORLD FASTER THAN EVER BEFORE, AND MAKE IT EASIER TO CREATE COLOURFUL AND EXCITING PUBLICATIONS.

GETTING INTO PRINT

History links

FAST WORK

FIRST THINGS FIRST

The text for this book was written using a word processor. The drawings were created on a computer. The complete package was put together on screen using page design software.

Producing a book, newspaper or magazine involves collecting an enormous amount of news and other information and turning it into an attractive printed publication.

Fast communications enable newspapers to be up-to-the-minute with their news coverage. Thanks to computers and telephones, text and pictures can be sent across the world in seconds by email or fax. This information is fed directly into the computerised page make-up systems that designers and editors use to produce the pages.

Editors of books and monthly magazines have more time than daily and weekly newspaper editors to produce each publication. They often receive text from authors and journalists on disk. But whether the text arrives by email, fax or disk, it is loaded into a word-processing program that enables it to be edited (changed) on the computer screen.

FIRST THINGS FIRST

Before the technology can be put to work, a great deal of planning is essential. An illustrated information book like this one begins with a synopsis – a list of the subjects that will appear on each page. The author writes the book on a word processor, then sends the text

30

GETTING INTO PRINT 31

by email or on a disk to the book's editor. The edited text is loaded into a computer that already holds a plan of the book's pages. The lengths of the lines are changed to fit the page design. In places where the text is too long, it has to be cut (shortened) to fit the space available for it. And if there is not enough text in other places, more has to be written.

Meanwhile, a picture researcher finds the photographs that will appear in the book. They may come from picture libraries, government departments or private companies. Or they may be photographed specially for the publication. An artist draws rough sketches of the illustrations for the editor and author to check before the final illustrations are produced.

The photographs and drawings are scanned into the computer and moved into place on the page plans. When all the text, photographs and drawings are in place on the computer screen, they are printed out for checking. Only when everyone is satisfied with the book is it sent for printing.

While a book is written and edited, the pictures are found and selected by a picture researcher.

History links

PAPERBACK BOOKS

Many books published today are paperback books. The paperback book became popular in the middle of the 19th century because it was quicker and less expensive to produce than leather- and fabric-bound books.

FAST WORK

The production of newspapers and magazines is slightly different. Writers all over the world may be supplying news stories and feature articles. Each contribution must be cut down to the right length for the space allocated to it. A picture editor or art editor selects photographs. They may have come from a picture library or they may just have been processed, having been taken earlier the same day. They may even have arrived in digital form by telephone. Newspapers and magazines also have to fit in advertisements. A whole department sells space and oversees the production of advertisements.

Photographers take pictures for publication in newspapers and magazines.

The text for this book was written using a word processor. The drawings were created on a computer. The complete package was put together on screen using page design software.

Producing a book, newspaper or magazine involves collecting an enormous amount of news and other information and turning it into an attractive printed publication.

Fast communications enable newspapers to be up-to-the-minute with their news coverage. Thanks to computers and telephones, text and pictures can be sent across the world in seconds by email or fax. This information is fed directly into the computerised page make-up systems that designers and editors use to produce the pages.

Editors of books and monthly magazines have more time than daily and weekly newspaper editors to produce each publication. They often receive text from authors and journalists on disk. But whether the text arrives by email, fax or disk, it is loaded into a word-processing program that enables it to be edited (changed) on the computer screen.

FIRST THINGS FIRST

Before the technology can be put to work, a great deal of planning is essential. An illustrated information book like this one begins with a synopsis – a list of the subjects that will appear on each page. The author writes the book on a word processor, then sends the text by email or on a disk to the book's editor. The edited text is loaded into a computer that already holds a plan of the book's pages. The lengths of the lines are changed to fit the page design. In places where the text is too long, it has to be cut (shortened) to fit the space available for it. And if there is not enough text in other places, more has to be written.

Meanwhile, a picture researcher finds the photographs that will appear in the book. They may come from picture libraries, government departments or private companies. Or they may be photographed specially for the publication. An artist draws rough sketches of the illustrations for the editor and author to check before the final illustrations are produced.

The photographs and drawings are scanned into the computer and moved into place on the page plans. When all the text, photographs and drawings are in place on the computer screen, they are printed out for checking. Only when everyone is satisfied with the book is it sent for printing.

History links

PAPERBACK BOOKS

Many books published today are paperback books. The paperback book became popular in the middle of the 19th century because it was quicker and less expensive to produce than leather- and fabric-bound books.

FAST WORK

The production of newspapers and magazines is slightly different. Writers all over the world may be supplying news stories and feature articles. Each contribution must be cut down to the right length for the space allocated to it. A picture editor or art editor selects photographs. They may have come from a picture library or they may just have been processed, having been taken earlier the same day. They may even have arrived in digital form by telephone. Newspapers and magazines also have to fit in advertisements. A whole department sells space and oversees the production of advertisements.

While a book is written and edited, the pictures are found and selected by a picture researcher.

Photographers take pictures for publication in newspapers and magazines.

MACHINE CODES

SOME PRINTED CODES ARE DESIGNED TO BE READ NOT BY PEOPLE, BUT BY MACHINES. SIMPLE PRINTED PATTERNS WHICH MEAN NOTHING TO THE CASUAL OBSERVER CAN HOLD IMPORTANT INFORMATION THAT A MACHINE CAN 'READ'. MACHINES ARE ALSO GETTING BETTER AT READING PRINTED AND HANDWRITTEN TEXT.

Next time you go shopping, have a good look at the item you are buying. Whether it's a bar of chocolate, a magazine or a packet of soap powder, you'll probably find a series of parallel black lines printed somewhere on the cover or the packet. The lines are a code, called a barcode, which is designed to be read by a computer. In large shops and supermarkets, all the products are passed in front of a red light at the check-out. The light scans across the lines, but it is reflected only by the white spaces between the lines. The on-off on-off code of reflections is detected by the system and changed into information that identifies the product and its manufacturer. The shop computer then looks up the product's price in its memory and sends the price back to the till.

The technology behind scanning has improved to the point where individual shoppers can now carry a handheld scanner around a shop with them and 'self-scan' goods as they are picked up off the shelves. Then, the prices of all the goods are downloaded from the hand scanner into the check-out till, greatly speeding up the check-out process. Many large supermarkets are beginning to use self-scanning technology.

Barcodes are also used in some airports for labelling baggage – ensuring that it goes to the right aircraft. And when you receive a parcel, you may find a barcode printed on it by the postal service or delivery company. The code is used to identify the parcel. When it is delivered, the code is scanned to register its delivery.

When shopping is passed through a supermarket check-out, a laser beam (the red lines) scans to and fro to pick up its barcode. The check-out computer bleeps when it detects the barcode.

A librarian uses a hand scanner to read a barcode on a borrower's library ticket and then scans the barcode on the book. Scanning both ticket and book enables the library's computer to store details of which book has been borrowed by which person.

Reading text

Ordinary alphabets are codes, too, but there are more characters and they're more complicated shapes than the lines in a supermarket barcode. So, they take more computer power to decode. There are two main ways in which a computer can 'read' printed text. First, an optical character recognition (OCR) system can read ordinary printed text. Secondly, text printed with magnetic inks can be detected by the magnetic fields it produces. Magnetic ink character recognition (MICR) systems are used in banks to read characters on cheques and bank drafts (see page 23).

Parcels often have to be signed for on delivery. Nowadays, you may find yourself signing the screen of a small, handheld computer or data logger. However, it is difficult for a computer to 'read' or 'understand' handwritten text because we all write differently. In 1988, the American company Scriptel introduced a system for inputting information into a computer by writing on the screen. In 1990, the Grid-Pad computer was invented, allowing users to input data by writing in capital letters on the screen. Future computers may not have keyboards at all, as handwriting recognition systems and voice recognition systems replace the keyboard as the standard way of communicating with a computer.

History links

LASER SHOPPING

The first laser barcode scanners were introduced in a small number of American supermarkets in 1974. By 1980, they were being installed in supermarkets worldwide.

Smart cards

Many of the records that used to be kept as print on paper are now capable of being stored in other, invisible ways – in solid-state memories. These solid-state memories can be as thin as paper and small enough to fit in a purse or wallet.

For centuries, information about people was kept in books and on record cards. The development of computers has resulted in billions of pieces of information about people being stored in a different way – in computer memories. Since the first PCs were introduced in the 1980s, computers have not only become faster and capable of storing more and more information, they have also become smaller. Each chip contains more individual electronic components than ever before. These developments have made it possible for all of us to carry digital information around in our pockets.

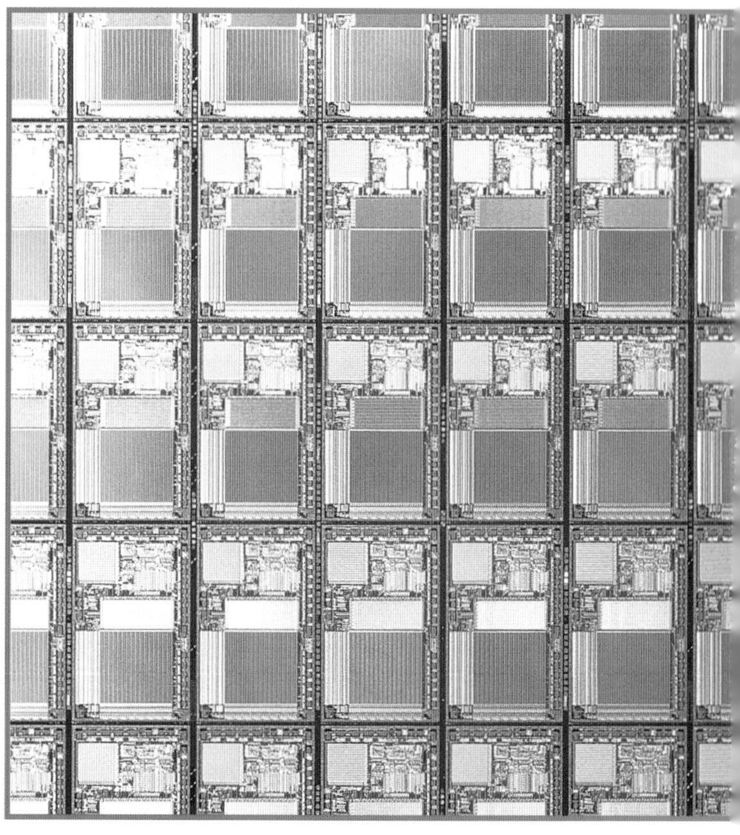

This is a type of chip called an EPROM (Erasable Programmable Read-Only Memory), and each individual square is a chip for a smart card. EPROMs are used because they can store information without power, such as batteries.

Magnetic data

Computers store data on magnetic disks. Floppy disks can be taken out of one computer and used in another, while hard disks are built into the computer. Both types store data by changing the way the material is magnetised. Look on the back of any cash card or credit card. There is a brown strip running the length of the card. This is a piece of material that can be magnetised just like a piece of recording tape or a computer disk. So, a plastic card can store details of a bank account or a credit card account. The information is 'printed' on the card magnetically – and invisibly.

Smart cards

A plastic card with a computer chip embedded inside it can do a lot more than one with a magnetic strip. These cards are known as smart cards. Some are memory cards containing a memory chip. Others are miniature computers with a central processing unit (CPU) as well as memory. Smart cards communicate with computers and communication systems in two ways. One type has to make contact with a reader. This type has gold contacts on the surface of the card. The other type has a wire coil aerial embedded in the card that can communicate with a reader some distance away by radio.

Banks and shops that issue loyalty cards are beginning to update their magnetic strip cards to smart cards. Telephone companies issue smart cards for buying call time on their telephone services. And smart cards can be used instead of cash. The card is loaded with money which is transferred from a bank account. Each time the card is used to pay for something in a shop, it is inserted in a terminal and the amount of money stored in the card is reduced. Smart cards can also be used to hold identification information.

The information stored electronically in the chip in a smart card can be changed, added to or erased whenever necessary. Today, the most common use of smart cards is for storing personal medical information.

Future uses of smart cards being developed and piloted in some parts of the world now include driving licences, passports, medical history records and tickets. Smart card tickets can be checked through a sports stadium door, a bus entrance or an airport terminal much faster than paper tickets, which have to be looked at or punched individually. A health or medical smart card could store not only the owner's medical history but also details of medicines currently prescribed and his or her organ donation wishes, family doctor details and next-of-kin details. Within the next few years, we will all be carrying smart cards for one reason or another.

VIRTUAL NEWSPAPERS

NEW TECHNOLOGY HAS ALREADY STREAMLINED THE WAY BOOKS, NEWSPAPERS AND MAGAZINES ARE PRINTED, BUT DEVELOPMENTS IN COMPUTERS AND COMMUNICATIONS COULD RADICALLY CHANGE THE APPEARANCE AND PRODUCTION OF FUTURE PUBLICATIONS.

Every time someone buys something and pays for it with a plastic card, a computer somewhere registers what has been bought and who has bought it. Supermarkets are developing systems that use this information to offer tempting discounts and attractive offers which are specially tailored to individual customers. In future, newspapers may use the same technology to produce newspapers that are specially compiled for each reader.

There are already virtual libraries on the World Wide Web. People can visit these libaries from anywhere in the world and search through books, magazines and newspapers. Anyone can download articles and stories that particularly interest them. In principle, the same software that analyses a shopper's habits could also analyse a reader's habits and put together a selection of the day's news stories. This selection would be tailored to that particular reader's preferences.

This technology opens the possibility of having individually adapted newspapers and magazines. Someone who isn't interested in sport would probably prefer to have only a page of the most important sports headlines. A doctor who plays rugby, enjoys foreign travel and collects clocks could have a newspaper or magazine that concentrates on those particular topics – health, medicine, rugby, travel and clocks, with perhaps just a short digest of all the other news and features that are available. These targeted newspapers could be sent directly to each reader's home by email and printed out by the reader's own computer.

Every day millions of people read newspapers. Tomorrow, on-line newspapers, constantly updated with the latest news, may be just as popular.

Newspapers and magazines are produced worldwide in every major language.

THE LANGUAGE BARRIER

Web sites often offer text in more than one language – just click on the language you want. But the choice is usually very limited – perhaps just English and the mother tongue of the web site producer. Computer software that can translate text from one language to another is available, but the technique is in its infancy.

Language, either spoken or printed, is a complicated pattern. Computers are very good at analysing patterns. As computer memories have continued to grow and their processing speeds increase, their language capabilities have developed, too. You can now buy an electronic translator that you wipe across printed text, like a pen, and the translation appears on its screen. So far, it can translate between English and French, German or Spanish. It stores almost half a million idioms for each language. In future, Web translators will be able to translate web sites from one language into another language in real-time as the text appears on the screen.

History links

THE WORLD WIDE WEB

The World Wide Web was invented between 1989 and 1992 by Tim Berners-Lee and others working at CERN, a European scientific organisation. The same team also created the hypertext transfer protocol (http), a set of standards that enables computers to exchange information.

VIRTUAL LIBRARIES

LIBRARIES USED TO BE BUILDINGS FULL OF BOOKS. TODAY, THEY LEND VIDEOS AND CDS AND OFFER ACCESS TO THE INTERNET, TOO. A NEW TYPE OF LIBRARY FOR THE FUTURE, A VIRTUAL LIBRARY, IS BEGINNING TO TAKE SHAPE. IT WILL STORE MILLIONS OF DIGITAL BOOKS, SOUND RECORDINGS AND VIDEO CLIPS.

The British Library must, by law, hold at least one copy of every book published in Britain. Its shelves contain 20 million books. Managing a collection of this size, and giving people access to any book, is a vast task. And, with thousands more books being published every year, the job is getting more difficult all the time.

The Library is tackling this by transferring some of its books into a digital form. Once a book is digitised, it can be stored in a computer and whizzed down the information superhighway to any other computer screen anywhere in the world within a few minutes. Digitisation not only enables people all over the world to access books, it also allows people to see books and other documents that are too old, too fragile or too valuable to be handled for real. Digital libraries will allow these books and documents, or at least images of them, to be seen by many more people.

The new British Library building in St Pancras, London, has almost 340km of shelf space for storing 25 million books and other documents. Readers can search for books and then request them using computer terminals in the library.

VIRTUAL BOOKS

The British Library has gone one step further than merely digitising books. It has created virtual books. What's the difference? The text and illustrations of a digitised book appear on a computer screen like the pages of a CD-ROM encyclopedia or pages of information accessed via the World Wide Web. You can

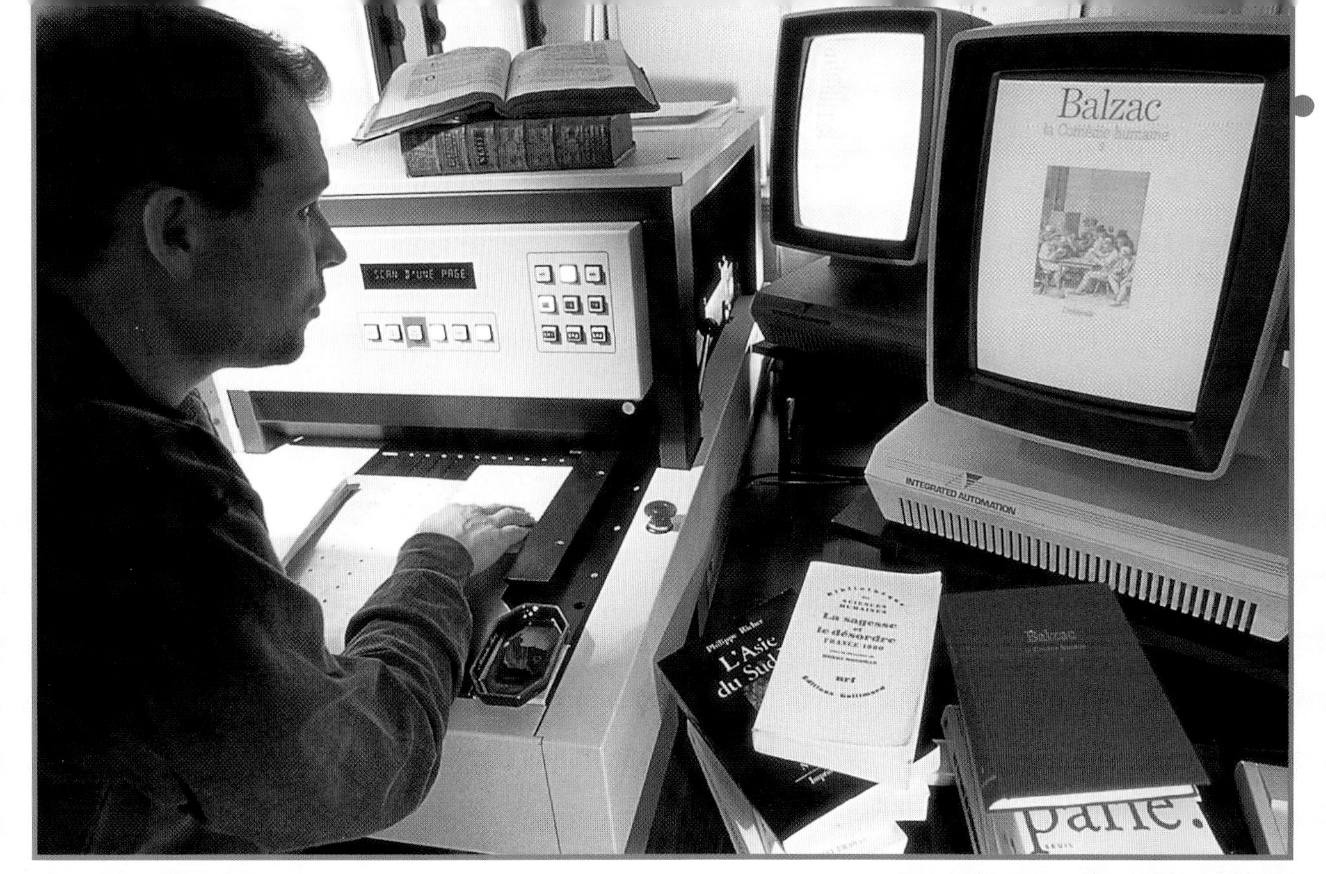

A technician scans a library book into a computer. The computer version can be distributed by CD-ROM or through a network such as the Internet. Virtual books enable more people to have access to rare and priceless books.

look further on in the text, or look back through it, by scrolling it up or down on the screen. A virtual book is different. Clever software makes it look like the real thing, a real book, and you can even turn its pages by hand! The screen of the British Library's virtual book is touch sensitive. When you run your fingers across the screen, as if turning the pages of a real book, the virtual book's pages turn too. Computer graphics show each page lifting, curling and flipping over to show the next page. The software even mimics the stiffness of the paper.

THE END OF PRINTED BOOKS?

Creating tens of millions of virtual books on CD-ROM is a mammoth task that will take years to complete. If more libraries follow the British Library's example, electronic books and virtual books will become more commonplace. Will publishers dispense with the printed book altogether and go straight to a digital format? There are already a few publishers, called on-line publishers, who publish books only on the World Wide Web. Printed copies of these books do not exist in any library or bookshop. But it is extremely unlikely that printed books will be completely replaced by digital books or virtual books. Printed books are portable, need no batteries, can be used anywhere without any extra equipment or software and they can be stored for years very easily and cheaply – on a bookshelf.

History links

NATIONAL LIBRARIES

Most developed countries have a national library whose job is to store and preserve the nation's books. The British Library is Britain's national library, equivalent to the Bibliothéque Nationale in France and the US Library of Congress. The British Library was founded as the British Museum Library in 1753. It was separated from the British Museum as recently as 1972.

MAP-MAKING

MAPS AND ATLASES ARE AMONGST THE MOST IMPORTANT PRINTED DOCUMENTS. THEY GUIDE PILOTS AND SAILORS ACROSS THE WORLD AND HELP DRIVERS TO FIND THEIR WAY THROUGH ROAD SYSTEMS. THEY RECORD THE LOCATIONS OF EVERYTHING FROM HISTORIC SITES TO POWER LINES. AND THEY SHOW THE PRECISE SIZE AND SHAPE OF PIECES OF LAND OWNED BY PEOPLE.

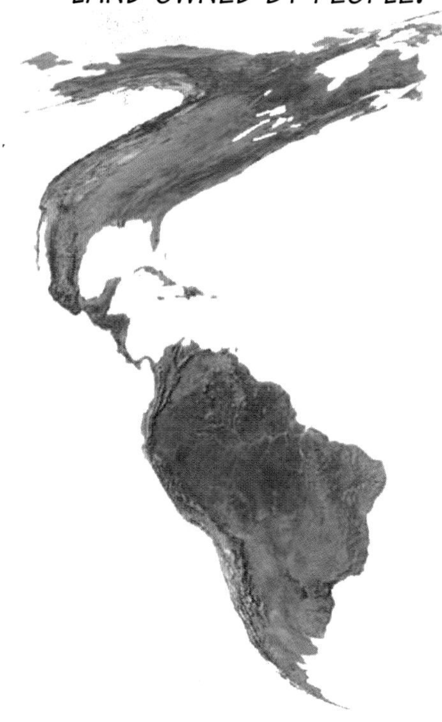

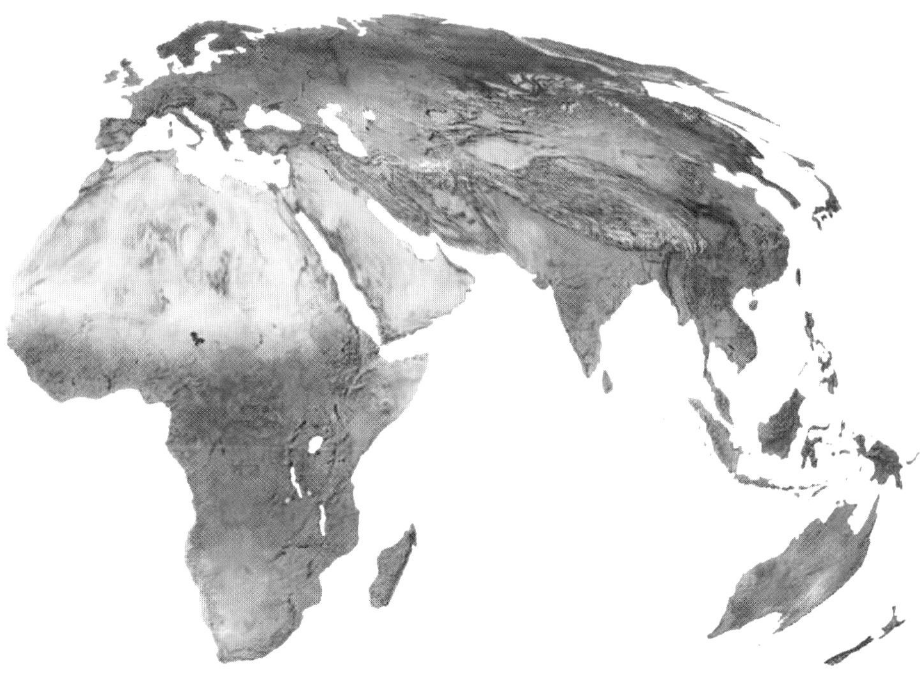

This view of the world has been pieced together from satellite pictures using a version of the Robinson map projection.

The first map-makers looked at the world around them, perhaps by walking the countryside or the streets of their town or by studying the coast of uncharted lands from a ship at sea, and recorded what they saw with pen and paper. This worked perfectly well for maps of small areas – but maps of bigger areas have a problem caused by the shape of the Earth.

ROUND INTO FLAT

The Earth is ball-shaped and three-dimensional, but maps are flat. How can a ball-shaped surface be turned into a flat map in an atlas? Map-makers solve the problem by using projections – so-called because points on the Earth are projected on to a flat surface. All projections distort the appearance of the Earth. The most popular projection used in most atlases and navigation charts is the Mercator projection, developed by Gerardus Mercator in 1569.

The Mercator projection enlarges countries near the poles – coincidentally mostly developed countries – making them look larger than countries near the Equator – mostly developing countries. Another projection, the Peters projection, shows countries in their correct proportions compared to each other, but it distorts their shapes. The Mercator projection has survived to the present day because a straight line in the real world appears as a straight line on Mercator maps, so navigators can use them to steer a course.

As all projections cause one type of distortion or another, one answer is to combine them all to create a new projection that produces the least distortion overall. This is a complicated job and it wasn't possible until computers were put to work on it. The result is a new projection called the optimal conformal projection. Maps made in this way are twice as accurate as any other maps.

Geographical images and information can be distributed via the Internet using computer programs that change them into Internet files.

COMPUTER-GENERATED MAPS

Computers have made possible an entirely new branch of information-processing that deals with maps, aerial photographs, satellite photographs and all sorts of surveying and mapping information. Geographical Information Systems (GIS) can take all of these different forms of information and combine them to produce highly detailed maps. Maps and ground-plans can be taken into the system, along with aerial photographs, re-scaled so that they are all the same size and layered on top of each other. This visual information can be linked to databases containing more information, such as population, plant, geology or weather data, so that clicking on a feature brings up the database on the screen. The maps and information can be sent anywhere by email or placed on a web site so that other people can access them.

Companies often have to work with different forms of geographical information, including very old maps drawn on paper, computer-generated maps, photographs, video images and geographical data. Some GIS computer programs can take in all these different forms of geographical information and combine them in different ways.

Timeline

BOOKS AND NEWSPAPERS DATES

WORLD DATES

BC

3000 The Egyptians invent papyrus, a paper-like writing material made from reeds.

2600 | Work begins on the Great Pyramid of Giza in ancient Egypt.

2500 Ink is invented in China.

776 | The first Olympic Games are held in Greece.

250 Parchment, treated animal skin is used for writing in Turkey.

215 | Construction work begins on the Great Wall of China.

150 Paper is invented in China.

79 | The volcano Vesuvius erupts and buries the city of Pompeii in ash.

AD

600 The Chinese print pages using wood blocks.

618 A court newspaper is printed in China.

635 The quill pen, made from a goose quill, is invented in Spain.

748 The first printed newspaper is produced in China.

868 The *Diamond Sutra*, the earliest known complete printed book is produced.

1000 | The Viking Leif Ericsson is the first European to land in North America.

1040 At about this time, Bi Sheng invents movable type (made from baked clay) in China.

1050 The first books are printed using movable type in China.

1066 | William the Conqueror lands in England and begins the Norman Conquest.

1107 Colour printing is invented in China to make paper money more difficult to copy.

1215 | The Magna Carta, the basis of English law, is written.

1271 | Marco Polo sets out from Venice on an epic journey to China.

1347 | Bubonic plague, spread by rat fleas, kills nearly half the population of Europe.

1390 Metal movable type is used in Korea.

1390 The first paper mill is built in Germany.

1447 Johann Gutenberg and Laurens Koster re-invent printing with movable type.

1454 Gutenberg prints the 42-line Bible at Mainz, in Germany – the first book to be printed with movable type in Europe.

1460 Albert Pfister combines woodcuts with movable type for the first time.

1465 The first book is printed in Italy.

1470 The first book is printed in France.

1474 William Caxton prints the first book in English.

1492 | Christopher Columbus discovers the West Indies while searching for a trade route to the Far East.

1494 The first paper mill is built in England.

1496 Music is printed for the first time.

1499 By this date, 20 million copies of 35,000 different books have been printed.

1520 The first book is printed in Africa.

1556 The first book is printed in India.

1564 The pencil is invented.

1569 The Mercator Projection, which is still used to print maps, is invented by Gerardus Mercator.

1606 | Dutchman Willen Jantszoon is the first European to reach Australia.

1638 The first printing press is set up in north America, at Cambridge, Massachesetts.

1642 | Abel Tasman becomes the first European to land on Tasmania.

1662 The Printing Act is passed by the English government to regulate what printers can print.

BOOKS AND NEWSPAPERS DATES

WORLD DATES

1666 The English government passes a law prohibiting people from being buried in cotton or linen shrouds because of a shortage of cloth rags for making paper.

1709 The first Copyright Act is passed in England, to protect an author's work from being copied.

1704 The first alphabetical encyclopedia in English is published.

1710 Three-colour printing is invented by Jacob Christoph Le Blon.

1714 The first typewriter is patented by Henry Mill in London.

1719 Four-colour printing is invented by Jacob Christoph Le Blon

1739 William Ged invents a printing method in which pages are printed from a lead plate. The plate is made from a papier-mâché mould, which is itself made from movable type. The plate can be used to print many copies.

1770 | Captain James Cook reaches Australia.

1771 The *Encyclopedia Britannica* is published for the first time.

1780 The first fountain pens are invented.

1783 | Joseph and Etienne Montgolfier build the first successful hot-air balloon.

1798 Lithography is invented by Alois Senefelder.

1796 | Edward Jenner carries out the first vaccination.

1800 The first iron printing press is built in London. Presses were previously made from wood.

1800 | Alessandro Volta invents the battery.

1802 | Richard Trevithick invents the steam locomotive.

1808 The first colour lithographs are produced.

1823 Firmin Gillot is the first person to print photographs by lithography.

1840 The first practical and successful typesetting machine is built.

1847 Richard March Hoe invents the rotary press and web printing.

1852 | Henri Giffard invents the airship.

1859 | Construction of the Suez Canal begins.

1872 Thomas Edison invents the electric typewriter.

1872 Christopher Latham Sholes invents the QWERTY keyboard layout.

1872 Charles Gillot invents photogravure printing.

1880 The first screened photographs, consisting of a grid of fine dots, are printed in the *New York Daily Graphic*.

1883 | The volcanic island Krakatoa explodes, making the loudest bang ever heard on Earth.

1884 Ottmar Mergenthaler invents the Linotype typesetting machine for casting metal 'slugs' containing entire lines of text for printing.

1884 Lewis Waterman invents the modern fountain pen.

1885 | Karl Benz builds the first modern petrol-engine motor car.

1887 Tolbert Lanston invents the Monotype typesetting machine.

1892 Thomas Oliver invents the first typewriter that allows the user to see words as they are typed.

1895 The first ballpoint pen is produced.

1902 The first successful electric typewriter is invented by George Blickensderfer.

1903 | Orville Wright makes the first sustained powered flight.

1904 Offset printing is invented by Ira Rubel.

1909 | Louis Blériot makes the first aeroplane flight across the English Channel

1912 | The passenger liner *Titanic* sinks in the North Atlantic Ocean.

1914-18 | World War I.

BOOKS AND NEWSPAPERS DATES

WORLD DATES

1915 The propelling pencil is invented by Rokuji Hayakawa.

1926 Robert Goddard launches the first liquid fuel rocket.

1927 Charles Lindbergh makes the first non-stop solo flight across the Atlantic Ocean.

1930 The planet Pluto is discovered by Clyde Tombaugh.
Frank Whittle invents the jet engine.

1935 The ink cartridge, invented in 1927, is patented by M. Perrand.

1936 The publisher Penguin introduces the modern paperback book.

1937 Chester Carlson invents xerography for copying documents.

1938 Lazlo Biró invents the first ballpoint pen to become a commercial success.

1939-45 World War II.

1947 Charles 'Chuck' Yeager makes the first supersonic flight in the experimental rocket-plane, the Bell X-1.

1949 The first modern photocomposition system is developed. It can set up to 50,000 characters per hour.

1953 Edmund Hillary and Tenzing Norgay climb the world's tallest mountain, Mount Everest, for the first time.
The structure of DNA is discovered by James Watson and Francis Crick.

1957 IBM invents the dot matrix printer.
The world's first artificial satellite is launched by the Soviet Union.

1959 The first commercial Xerox copying machine goes on sale.

1961 IBM introduces the golf-ball typewriter.
Cosmonaut Yuri Gagarin becomes the first human being to orbit the Earth, in Vostok 1.

1963 The felt-tipped pen is invented by the Japanese pen manufacturing company Pentel.

1966 The daisywheel computer printer is invented.

1967 Christiann Barnard performs the first heart transplant, in South Africa.

1969 The first human being walks on the moon, Apollo 11 astronaut Neil Armstrong.

1970 The first Jumbo Jet enters service.

1971 The first Intel microprocessor is introduced.
The first space station, Salyut 1, is launched.

1973 The Skylab space station is launched.

1974 The first scanners capable of reading barcodes are introduced in US supermarkets.

1975 IBM invents the laser printer.

1976 IBM invents the inkjet printer.

1978 The first test tube baby, Louise Brown, is born.

1980 The wreck of the passenger liner *Titanic* is discovered,

1981 The US Space Shuttle is launched for the first time.

1985 Rodger Gamblin invents a printing ink that does not run or stain readers' fingers.

1986 The Mir space station is launched.
The nuclear reactor at Chernobyl explodes.

1990 Nelson Mandela is released from prison in South Africa.

1991 The *New York Times* begins printing using a new type of ink that does not rub off on readers' hands.

1997 Andy Green sets the first super sonic land speed record in Thrust SSC.

Glossary

BLANKET CYLINDER A rubber-covered roller used in an offset printing press to transfer an inked image from a printing plate to an impression cylinder.

COLLATING Arranging pages into their correct number order.

FLEXOGRAPHY A type of letterpress printing that uses a flexible rubber printing plate and quick-drying inks.

FLONG A soft sheet of pasteboard used to make a printing plate for a rotary relief press.

FORME The frame into which a typesetter locks type in a flatbed relief printing press.

FOUNT Also called font – a complete set of characters of a certain style and size used in printing.

GRAVURE A printing method using a printing plate with tiny pits etched in its surface to hold the ink.

HARD COPY A print-out on paper from a computer.

HOT METAL PRINTING A printing method that uses printing plates cast from molten metal.

IMPRESSION CYLINDER A rubber-covered roller used in an offset printing press to transfer an image on to the paper.

INKJET A printing method that works by spraying droplets of ink.

INTAGLIO PRINTING A printing method such as gravure in which the inked part of the printing plate is recessed below the surface of the plate, usually by being etched with acid.

LEADING The spacing between lines of print, named after the strips of lead that printers used to space out lines of type.

LETTERPRESS A printing method in which the printing part of a printing plate is raised above the rest of the plate, usually by etching the non-printing parts of the plate with acid.

LITHOGRAPHY A printing method that uses a flat printing plate, on which the printing part is covered by greasy ink and the non-printing part is moistened with water.

MOVABLE TYPE Individual characters cast as separate pieces of metal, called type, so that they can be arranged in any order.

OFFSET PRINTING A printing method that transfers, or offsets, the image to be printed on to a roller, or cylinder, before it is printed on the paper.

PLATEN The flat metal plate in a platen press that presses the paper against the raised type.

PLATEN PRESS A type of printing press in which the paper is raised up and pressed against the type.

RELIEF PRINTING A printing method in which the inked part of the printing plate stands higher than the rest of the plate.

ROTARY PRESS A printing press which prints on paper passing through a pair of rotating rollers.

ROTOGRAVURE Printing using a rotary gravure press.

SHEET-FED PRESS A printing press that prints on separate sheets of paper.

TYPEFACE The style and size of a set of characters used in printing. There are hundreds of typefaces, for example Times Roman, Arial and Helvetica.

TYPESETTING Arranging type to form text that will be printed.

WEB A continuous strip of paper supplied to a printing press from a giant roll.

WEB OFFSET PRESS A type of printing press that prints on a continuous strip of paper, by transferring, or offsetting, the image on to a cylinder called a blanket before printing it on the paper.

INDEX

Internet links

You can find out more about some of the subjects in this book by looking at the following web sites:

http://www.heidelberg.com
(Printing press manufacturer)

http://www.bnf.fr
(Bibliothèque Nationale, France)

http://www.bl.uk
(The British Library, UK)

http://lcweb.loc.gov
(US Library of Congress)

http://.eb.co.uk
(Encyclopedia Britannica)

http://www.mondexusa.com
http://www.smartcrd.com/info/whatis/faq.htm
(Smart cards)

http://wwwiicink.com/prods.html
(Specialist ink manufacturer)

http://warren-idea-exchange.com
(Graphic arts, paper-making and printing)

http://home.vicnet.net.au/~conserv/prepast1.htm
(Book conservation)